Creature abc

Andrew Zuckerman

chronicle books · san francisco

p

Creature ABC first published in the United States in 2009
by Chronicle Books LLC.

Hippopotamus, Penguins, Porcupine 1, Vulture, and Oryx images
© 2009 by Andrew Zuckerman.
All other images © 2007 by Andrew Zuckerman, from *Creature*
published by Chronicle Books.

Library of Congress Cataloging-in-Publication Data available.

ISBN 978-0-8118-6978-2

Book design by David Meredith.

Manufactured in China.

Produced and originated by PQ Blackwell Limited
116 Symonds Street, Auckland, New Zealand
www.pqblackwell.com

10 9 8 7 6 5 4 3 2 1

Chronicle Books LLC
680 Second Street
San Francisco, California 94107

www.chroniclekids.com

To Ethan

Aa

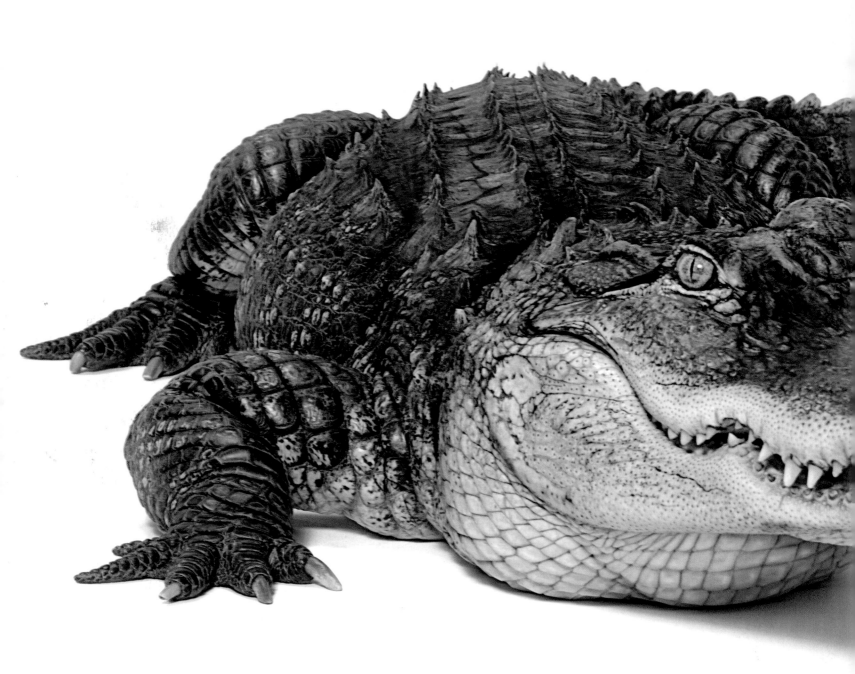

alligator

Bb

bear

Cc

chameleon

Dd

dove

Ee

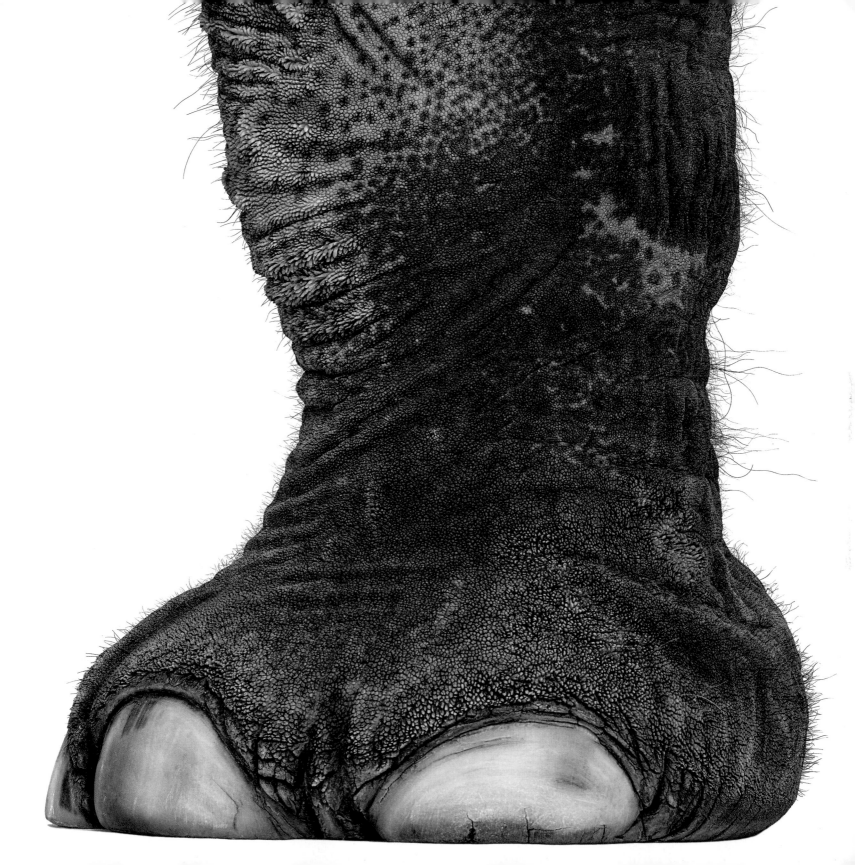

elephant

Ff

frog

Gg

giraffe

hippopotamus

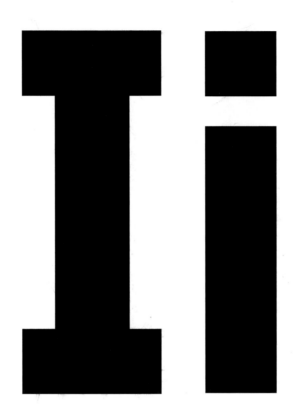

beetle

grasshopper

bee

insect

ant

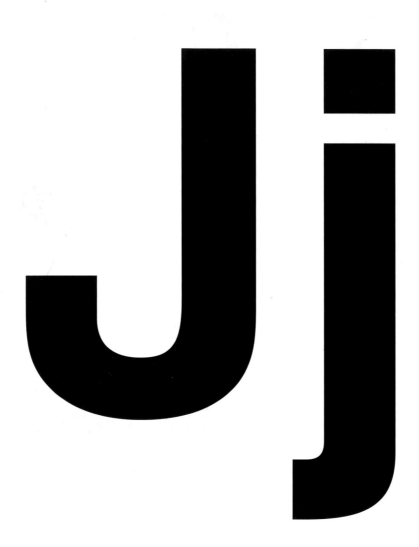

jackrabbit

Kk

kangaroo

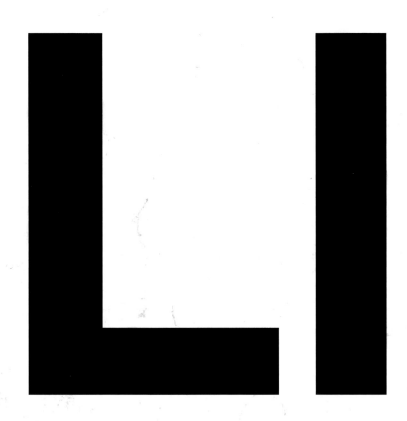

lion

M

mandrill

American badger

bat

nocturnal

slow loris

Oo

owl

Pp

penguin

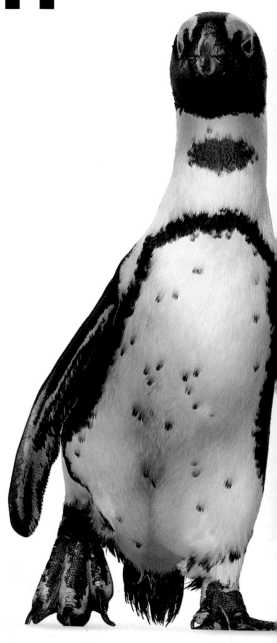

Qq

quills

rooster

Ss

scorpion

tiger

Uu

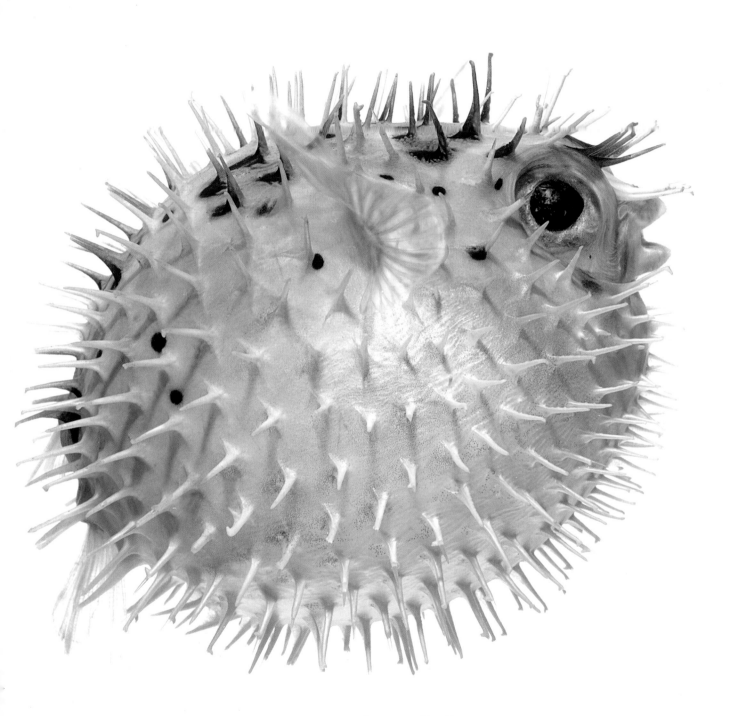

porcupine fish

goldfish

underwater

arowana

koi

Vv

vulture

Ww

wolf

oryx

Yy

yellow canary

zebra

Glossary

Aa
Half of an alligator's length is its huge, powerful tail. When babies hatch, their mother carries them to the water in her mouth.

Bb
Black bears actually come in a variety of colors. They can be black, brown, cinnamon, blond, blue-gray, or even white.

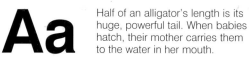

Ff
Red-eyed tree frogs eat flies, grasshoppers, and even smaller frogs. During the day, they close their bright eyes to better camouflage themselves.

Gg
Giraffes have long necks so they can scan the African grasslands for predators while they munch on treetops. No two have the same spots.

Jj
Jackrabbits, also called hares, can run up to 45 miles per hour and jump as high as 10 feet.

Kk
When running from a predator, red kangaroos can jump 25 to 40 feet in a single bound. They use their giant, powerful tails for steering and balance.

Ll
The male lion's mane helps him look fierce so that he can scare away other lions. His roar can be heard up to 5 miles away.

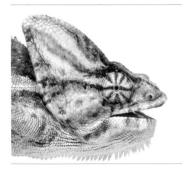

Cc A chameleon can move each eye in a different direction at the same time and shoot its tongue out half its body length.

Dd The dove, a type of pigeon, can be taught to carry important messages and can fly as fast as 44 miles per hour.

Ee The Asian elephant's trunk has over 100,000 muscles and makes sounds that can be heard 10 miles away.

Hh The hippopotamus spends most of its day in the water in order to stay cool in the hot climate. It also sweats a special oil that acts as a "hippo sunscreen."

Ii More than half of known living organisms are insects. There are well over a million species of insects on Earth.

Mm Mandrills with the brightest colors on their faces and backsides are the leaders so that their family can follow them through the rain forest.

Nn Nocturnal animals are active at night and sleep during the day. They usually have highly developed senses of hearing and smell, and specially adapted eyesight.

Glossary

Oo
Screech owls like to live in hollow trees. They hunt for insects, reptiles, and small mammals and will even dive into shallow waters to catch crayfish.

Pp
Penguins have strong wings for swimming and diving, but they can't fly. Penguins also make good parents, with males and females taking turns caring for chicks.

Ss
The emperor scorpion lives in burrows under rocks in the hot deserts of Africa. Babies ride on their mother's back until they are old enough to hunt on their own.

Tt
Baby tigers begin following their mother out of the den around eight weeks old. At two to three years old, they leave to find their own territory.

 Ww
Gray wolves often communicate through body language such as baring their teeth and raising their ears to show anger, or waving their tails and dancing around when they want to play.

 Xx
The oryx lives in the African grasslands. Both males and females have two horns that are about ½-meter long.

Qq

The quills of a porcupine are actually hollow hairs that are raised in defense against predators. Porcupines have as many as 30,000 quills covering the entire body except the stomach.

Rr

Roosters like to crow to announce the dawn, but they can also cluck like hens. The fleshy red part on top of its head is called a comb.

Uu

Oceans cover more than 70 percent of the Earth's surface. There are more than 25,000 species of fish in the waters of our planet.

Vv

Vultures are found on every continent except for Australia and Antarctica. They have bald heads to help regulate their body temperature.

Yy

Yellow canaries are known for their beautiful singing voices. In the wild, they eat weeds, grasses, and figs.

Zz

Zebras live in large groups called herds and eat bark, leaves, fruit, and roots. A zebra's teeth keep growing for its entire life because constant eating wears them down.